LIFE WITHOUT

YOU

By

I. L. Grady

For my daughters De'Ja and Jalissa, and

my sisters Yvette and LaVette.

Dedication

In honor of my wonderful brother Devorak Ladrakier Grady, who passed away on July 10, 2023 (he was born on September 18, 1962).

Never a day goes by that I don't think about you. I chat with you while gazing up at the sky and am aware of your presence in the wind's nudges. When I close my eyes, you are there, always grinning and radiating love at me.

I appreciate you being my mentor and teaching me the genuine meaning of experiencing life to the fullest. Through your example, I gained insight into the importance of tenacity and the power of resilience. Your unshakable courage will always inspire me to face challenges and adversities.

Even if you aren't physically present with us, your memory endures in our special times together. You have left a permanent imprint on my heart, and I will always carry your love with me.

This book is a celebration of your unwavering character and your enormous influence on my life. You will always be in our hearts; we will never forget you. And I will follow your example as I navigate life.

My beloved brother, you are loved.

With love and gratitude forever!

Acknowledgments

First, I must thank GOD for his guidance and assistance. I am nothing without you.

To my daughter, De'Ja, you have made me proud of you with your strengths. Nothing you could do could lessen what I feel for you. I love you, my baby girl!

To Jeffery, Jalissa, and Terry, I am honored that you find me fit to call me mom. You have made me proud. Always remember to listen to your voice. I love you big time!

Cindy, you know who you are. You are my biggest fan, and I thank you for sitting down and reading my life. Thanks for putting in the time to read me. Everything I write is me, and not once did you judge me. You know my secrets; thank you for keeping them in your heart. Smiling – my lips are sealed. Thanks for believing in me.

To my mother, you are the reason why I love to write. My first poems were an expression of my love for you.

To my girls, remember who the most important person in the world is—you!

Russell: You walked me through my first book. I could not have made it without you. You are my SUPERHERO.

To all the people I did not name, I hold you close to my heart. Thank you for loving me on the days when I didn't want to be loved.

I.L. Grady

Prologue

I made a terrible mistake. Actually, my heart did. It stops beating. The minute, the man I loved. The man I loved was my second thought. First thought, God. He told me his truth. He loudly said I don't love you. I like you. WOW! What a way to convey your feelings. We had no conversation. I just sat there frozen in time; nothing moved. I refused to cry. He did not care that my heart was broken. I will not cry in front of him. I will not give him that. He said what he had to say and had no trouble saying it. I can't sleep at night. Going to bed with his body next to mine made no sense. The old things that made so much sense made none; underneath the cover, I would silently cry. His touch meant nothing. His words meant nothing to him, at least.

Everything was just a habit to him. I believed in him. I believed in the US. There is no us. He gave me everything. I don't want to sleep for the fear I might dream. Dreaming is not in our future anymore. He gave me everything I wanted. It was me, him, and God. I don't know him. He is unrecognizable. I could never imagine that the only man I loved liked me. I love him, and it hurts.

How beautiful it is to find someone

who asks for nothing,

but your company.

--Briggitte Nicole--

Ryland was that friend that made me smile. For two years, he was my good company. When I felt like I wanted to cry, he would remind me how ugly I looked when I did. On his bad days, we would eat Popeye's Chicken, comfort food for him. We would sit, eat, and watch people walk by. "Everybody has a comfort place," he said.

For two years, he has listened to me without judging me. He shared his life, and I shared mine. He was my friend. I knew in my heart that he would be my forever and ever friend.

Since meeting him, we made a point to do small things that mattered to us. We had lunch, and sometimes we just ate quietly. No words. Sharing a banana split at Dairy Queen was our calming time.

We would sit at the highest point of Wahiawa, and looking down the mountain was absolutely breathtaking. Every day, there was a rainbow. Every day, we were part of it.

Ryland was my friend, and he knew it.

I often sit back and think about how I got to where I am today—life without him. Repeat! I think about hearing those words. I like you. I like you. As sweet and gentle as those words are, they are cold to the touch in my heart and mind. I wanted the like to be loved, but it wasn't. He didn't say I love you; he said, "Oh, I don't love you. I only like you." He would tell me to get a life. Wow!

I held my tears. I refused to let him see me cry—not today. I patiently waited for him to go to our bedroom. Then, I went into the TV room and cried. You see, he was my air. However, I was suffocating, and I was dying.

You know in your heart who that most important person is. He was my second thought. My first thought was GOD. I am at a loss. I can't breathe. I can't talk. I am broken!

It is true; you can't put Humpty Dumpty back together. He broke me.

I am broken!

It's not always just the heart.

Sometimes your

mind breaks as well.

~R. H. Sin

Jaiden

On one of the mornings, I was walking and not knowing where I was going. I must admit I took his credit card and made myself feel good. As he walked out the door, saying "I love you" to him didn't make sense. Typically, one would say, "I love you," and then he would reply, "I love you, too." Well, I said nothing.

I got up and prepped the kids for school. Yes, kids. We, me, the man that liked me, adopted my two nieces as our own—legally, committed to two kids. We went to court, and we talked to a judge. We made a vow to these kids. To be their forever and ever. You know the man that liked me? If he didn't love me, I knew he loved those kids. Both kids were our breath of fresh air. I thank God for them.

I thought about the person I used to be before I met him. I missed her dearly. I didn't realize who I was and what I had become of myself until that day. I changed for him.

I CHANGED FOR HIM!

I remembered who I was and the game of life. At this very moment, life has changed for me. It was now true to the game, as they say. Here we go, or here I go. My mission has begun. I am trying to get back to who I am.

Wait a minute. Who am I? The wife. It is a full-time job, and I assure you, I don't get paid for my overtime. I only know how to be his at this time. He chose me. He put that damn wedding dress on our bed, with our wedding rings, and I accepted the job. I changed myself, being the woman he wanted me to be.

Every day, he laid out my clothes and the girls' clothes. I was expected to walk a certain way. Talk a certain way. There was an expectation that I was expected to live by. And you know what? Even though I didn't agree with most of it, I did it because I loved him. Not like him.

5

As I walked Wilikina Drive, I stopped at a boutique that caught my attention. I walked into the boutique and saw the me I used to be. I tried on outfit after outfit, and when I walked out, I had a new one for each day of the week. I found a salon and waited hours for my hair to be done. I let my bun down, and the stylist worked her magic on me. I couldn't remember when was the last time I had my hair down. It was at my waist, and I felt alive.

I had spent money I would normally not spend. I walked back home, expecting the unknown. When the man who liked me walked in, I was looking out the patio door. I guess I was trying to put myself in a different place.

"Genie, where are you?" I thought. "Please invite me into your bottle."

Every day, he did the same thing. He would walk in, take off his boots at the door, take the same 19 steps, and make a quick right into the living room. He does this EVERY DAY! After he took that sharp right on that day, he asked me if I knew where Reece was. I turned around, and he was stuck. He was shocked.

It was me, and I was no longer the me he wanted me to be. Remember, he dressed me every day. Today, I dressed myself. Today, I became me again.

I am not sure what was going on in his mind. I only know when he realized who I was. There were no words for him. His mouth was closed.

I was conscientious about how I dealt with him. I did what I was expected to do. I cooked him dinner and made his plate. I even ran his bath today and laid the towels out for him. I laid his uniform out for the next day. The one thing I could not change was that I was his wife.

I called my mother, crying. She asked, "Is the house clean? Is there food in the house? Are the kids taken care of? Have you done what a wife is supposed to do?"

I replied, "Yes, ma'am."

She said, "Then there is nothing he can do."

I stopped crying. I was content, at least for the moment. I helped the girls with math and fed them.

I told him I was going out. I did not wait for him to reply. There was nothing he could say to me that would change the way I felt.

I was suffocating.

I was dying.

I was the wife.

It hurts, it hurts, I'm dying, and I'm dying.

~Herve Villechaize

Ryland

Ryland has a smile that melts your heart. I remember the day I met him. He was dressed all in black—leather pants, a leather vest, and a white shirt. I had on all white … We were on a Mason's Black and White cruise. I had been invited by my neighbor, Jackie. It was supposed to be the two of us, but I was the third wheel. I was standing on the ship's top deck looking out at the sun's setting, realizing I was on a cruise alone. Ryland approached me, and what got my attention was that smile. I couldn't speak. I just smiled back. He introduced himself to me. He said, "Hello, my name is Ryland Maize."

I said, "Hi, my name is Edris."

We walked the whole ship and shared a little about each other. I said I was from Kansas, and he told me he was from Virginia. I shared with him that I was married, and my husband had just shared that he liked me. That he wanted me, not loved me. To my surprise, he said, "You are loved, Edris."

WOW!!! I am loved. We heard the Hawaiian music playing and decided to see what was happening. It was locals dancing their native dance, and they asked for people to join them. He pushed me to join them. I first refused, and then I went on stage. Why not? No one knew me but my neighbor, who was in her man's arms. Ryland walked me to the stage. He grabbed my arm and told me, "You are beautiful."

I blushed, and at that moment, I felt beautiful. I felt the warmth of the sun that had already set. I was in Hawaii; I was on a cruise, and a total stranger had told me I was beautiful. He had made my day. No, he had woken up the sad side of me, and I knew I had found a friend. At least, I had hoped. I danced the hula I had been practicing in the mirror at home. Surprisingly, I did great; that's what I told myself. I gained confidence, and I smiled. I met a handsome man with a smile that made me smile. It was perfect.

9

After the dance, we found ourselves sitting at the round table. Everyone was dressed in black and white. I remember eating Mahi Mahi and him eating a chicken dish of some sort. We talked about the people in our lives who meant something to us. We made a toast to new friendships. I must admit I didn't think about my husband, that man that "liked me." I heard the chime of the ship. It was a sound that the ship made to let you know that we were about to come to shore.

I felt, kind of, empty. The reality was about to slap me right in the face. I found Jackie, and of course, she was smiling. I was again the third wheel. I told Ryland bye and walked behind Jackie, smiling and happy she had invited me. Once I disembarked the ship, Ryland approached me and said, "Do you have a pen? I want to give you my number."

I said, "No! But I have a photographic memory."

He said, "808-555-4298."

"808-555-4298." I smiled, and I repeated his phone number.

I got it. He smiled and said, "Please call me."

I got in the backseat of Jackie's car, and I thought about how much fun I had. I got to dress up, and I got to dance the hula. I got to go on a cruise and eat Mahi Mahi. The best part was that I met a man with a beautiful smile who told me I was beautiful and loved—not liked. I rode home in the back of Jackie's car. In my head, I was singing 808-555-4298. I know the number, and singing it was music to my ears. The ride home was quiet for me. I was in the back singing to myself, and Jackie was in the front seat content. She was humming I love me some Him. In my head, I said it must be nice to feel that. "I love me some Him," too. Helll, lovvve, like lovvve like.

I am still out done that my husband would wait until he gets me 5,000 miles over the Pacific Ocean to say I like you. Really? I like you. When he told me, I was sitting on the couch waiting for him to come home. He stopped beside me with his briefcase and said bluntly, "I don't love you. I like you."

I didn't know what to say. I said nothing inside. I was crying. I refuse to let him see me cry. I waited until he went to the bedroom, and I went to the TV room, and I cried my eyes out. I am here in Hawaii, with no family alone, and my husband tells me he likes me. I guess he didn't know he was my air. I was suffocating, and I was dying. I loved him. I am CRUSHED.

It was because I was suffocating and dying that I had Jade. I think it was God giving me another lease on life. He gave me a life, and I had to live the life he blessed me. Right? In my mind, I say that Ryland didn't mean anything to me. We were just friends. I tell that to myself every day.

I remember that Saturday as if it was yesterday. Ryland had called me to let me know he was back from Haiti, just as he had before he left. That was something he gave me. He always let me know his whereabouts. I met him at the front gate. He had promised that he would take me around the island when he returned. He did just that. I got in his BMW and drove to the National Memorial Cemetery. As we walked through the cemetery, we saw families sitting down and eating with their deceased family. The children were running around playing. It was a peaceful moment. No one has died. They were just visiting. It was a beautiful place. Everything was white against the green.

Later, we went to the Lanai lookout located on the North Shore. Our goal was to make it around the island and see as many places as possible. He had told me that his heart was broken and that the woman he invested so much into had left him empty. I had no words for him. I knew how he felt because I had walked in his shoes not so long ago. In Diamond Head, we passed Pearl Harbor, sat down, and listened to the waterfall in Manoa. For lunch, we found McDonalds, and I had Ramen noodles and rice.

I. L. Grady

I had never been to his place, so we decided to talk there. Everything In his house was white. Everything was just white—white carpet, white couch. He had this fertility mask hanging on his wall that caught my eye. Now, I think I probably should not have looked at that. From every place he had ever been to, he had artifacts. The mask was from Haiti, and the elephants were from Japan. The pictures were from Korea. We sat down, and he told me his pain. A part of me felt sorry for him because she had no idea she lost a good man. He poured me a glass of red wine. We toast to life.

Halfway through the bottle, the phone rang. I'm not sure who was on the phone with him, but I kissed him anyway, hoping to distract his attention from the call. I was playing with him, and I am sure he would never kiss me back. Nothing would have changed. Right? He hung up the phone, and he kissed me back. I didn't push him away. I didn't say a word. He pulled me close, and I followed him to his perfect room. He undressed me perfectly. I watched him as he undressed. He kissed me and showered me with love; we said nothing. He was my friend, and my heart told me so. He took me to the gate, and I went home.

My mind is not at ease. I had done the unthinkable to some. There was no right in this wrong, but it felt good. I had no regrets. For the most part, my days were pleasant. I got up every day for work. I cleaned the house. I cooked the food. I washed the clothes. I smiled because I needed to. Remember, I am in love, and he is in the like.

This couple of weeks have been different. I am living life the best I can. I still run 5 miles daily—two and a half miles in the morning and two and a half miles in the evening. I am just trying to get fit with Oprah. I just finished my run, and my sister is waiting for me at the finish line. She was supposed to run with me, but that didn't happen.

I casually told her I had missed my period. She kept quiet. I asked her to walk to the PX with me, and she did. In my head, I was trying to remember my last period. Maybe I forgot. In my head, I knew I had counted right. Every 28 days, I had one. I know my cycle. I had missed it. WOW! The best part is whatever it is. At least I am not pregnant.

My doctor told me I could never get pregnant. Maybe it's my eating habits. Maybe it is my ulcers or the stress of life.

We walked to the PX, and I went to the downstairs bathroom. I read the directions, and I took the test. It was the longest three minutes of my life. I looked at the test, and I got sick to my stomach. I was pregnant. And the father of my child is not my husband. The one who liked me did not love me. My day didn't change. Being pregnant by another man did not change the person I am. I woke up every day. I cooked every day. I got the girls off to school every day. I am losing myself every day. I have no answer, but I am not worried. I am crushed. This was not supposed to be part of my life.

My days became transparent. I was in my office at home when I heard the phone ring. It was Ryland. I listened to his voice and smiled at my friend who had called me, and I had missed him. I didn't know what to say. So, I listened to his words. Our conversation was the same. However, my heart was beating faster than usual. I had something to tell him. We talked about our day. He made his jokes, and I laughed. Then he asked me, "Why Haven't you been calling me?"

I said, "I am pregnant."

He was silent and then said, "I figured that."

I couldn't say anything, and I had no words. I was stuck. We continued talking as if I had said nothing. He didn't question me. The fact that he was so normal scared me. I just told my friend that I was pregnant by him. The only thing he said was I figured that. WHAT!

I hung up the phone, and I lay down. I had no thoughts. I know that I would have this child. Every morning, I ran my 2.5 miles. Every evening, I did the same thing. I was carrying another man's baby. I had no time to be afraid. I had to reach deep down into my soul and find ME.

A few days passed when I saw Ryland pull up to my car. I was waiting for Jaiden to come home. He had just got back from Treasure Island in California. If I had ever been scared, it was today. Ryland pulled up to my house and left a letter on my car.

My husband was on his way home. At that moment, I began to sweat. My heart was beating fast. I couldn't even form the words to ask why you are here. Fear had hit me; it knocked me out. I gathered my thoughts, and I ran downstairs.

He was gone. I took the letter out of my car and went upstairs to read it. My hands were shaking, and I could not open the letter. I put it underneath my bed, and I walked away. Within minutes, Jaiden walked through the door. He was talking about a narrow escape. It took me three days to read that letter. In a nutshell, he said, he was close to retirement. He thought I had trapped him. He didn't want any more children. Yes! He has a 7-year-old daughter. He had worked hard to get where he was and did not want to lose everything he worked for. I read that letter several times. Each time I read it, I got mad. Each time I read it, I was sad. Then, it was a part of me that was happy. I am carrying a child that I wanted. How can I be sad? I have a life inside of me.

Ryland was my friend. He, within weeks of our actions, abandoned me. I think whatever you do in life, there is a cost involved, whether it be a good deed that makes you smile or whether that it be a bad deed that makes you cry. The choice of doing what is right is solely based on your efforts. It is true, sometimes, that you can't worry about the hurt.

I have had sleepless nights since I received the letter from Ryland. I wished he had mailed me that letter. Maybe I should have written, return to sender. I understand how he is feeling. Does he care how I am feeling? I am empty.

"Ask and it will be given to you; seek and you will find; knock and the door will be opened to you. For everyone who asks receives; the one who seeks finds; and to the one who knocks, the door will be opened."

(Matthew7:7-8).

Ryland

Forgive me, Lord. I didn't ask.

No one sees how broken I really am.

~unknown

That was the last time I saw Ryland. I had lost my friend. I was in acute coronary syndrome. No, I am fine. I am just waiting to wake up from this bad dream.

Damn, in a matter of months, I lost a husband and gained a friend. Then, I lost a husband, lost a friend, and earned a baby. A part of me is at ease. I am not worried.

Jaiden walked in from work, and I just told him I was pregnant. I didn't stutter. I didn't walk away. I stood there waiting on the rapture. It never happened. He just said, "okay."

I believe that at that moment, I had to pinch myself. Edris, are you sleeping? Wake the hell up! I just told my husband, who has been gone for months, that I was pregnant, and all he said was, "Okay!"

Well, okay. I entered the living room, and he went upstairs to his office. Later, I got dressed, and I went for a run. I thought about my friend, who I missed dearly. I thought about this baby and how life would be as it grew inside me.

Ryland walked away from me, and I understood. I over stood. I am not sure how I trapped him. I think it must have been that red wine. I want to be drinking again.

Jaiden never asked for paternity. He knew this child was not his. At the moment, it didn't matter. Ryland had saved me. The day I met him, he saved me. He gave me everything I needed. I was suffocating; he breathed into me that I was dying and pushed me to live. I was broken, and he helped put me back together.

I wasn't in love with him. He was my pretend drill sergeant. I was his soldier. He taught me *loyalty. Bear true faith and allegiance to the Constitution, the Army, your unit, and other soldiers. Duty fulfills your obligations. Respect. Selfless service. Honor. Integrity. Personal Courage.*

He taught me the Army core, which I applied in my life. I am army-strong. It is something about standing tall when you are only 4'11". In my mind, I am 6 feet tall, and I owe that all to him.

Ryland was not my lover. He was my friend. One sweet moment, we kissed, and he became human. He pulled me close, took me into his perfectness, and I followed.

Before that night, we had never touched. I never kissed; we never became one.

One night, life took a turn, and there was a cost. Loneliness. Hmmm, wine couldn't fix that. We crossed the line, and it cost me, not him.

I called Ryland, and he was not home. I left a message telling him I would not have the baby and everything would be okay. I told him I was going to get an abortion. I lied. I told him I never wanted to see him again. I lied. I cried.

As small as the island was, I never saw him again. I am pregnant, and although this should be the happiest time of my life, I am sad.

I continue to run my 5 miles a day—my saving grace. I watch what I eat. I spend time with my nieces and play the fake wife with my husband.

My love for him has changed. Love and liking are hurtful things in a marriage. He doesn't ask about the baby. I don't talk about the baby. I did my wifely duties. I make love to him as a wife should. Falling out of love with him was not easy. He was my air, and he broke me.

Now, I am breathing, thanks to Ryland. I am living life thanks to Ryland.

Jaiden has been getting TDY in California for six months. Wow, about the time he gets back, the baby will be here. We pack, sign insurance papers, and go shopping for the things needed in the home.

We take the girls to the beach. We come home. We say our goodbyes and watch him leave until we can't see him anymore. He will call me once he makes it.

Smiling, I am going to be a mother. I will bring life into this world and be complete. My months of being pregnant were routine. I went to work, and I ran. I came home and cooked for the girls and then ran. Jaiden called every night at the same time to talk to the girls. Then we went to bed and started over.

When Jaiden came home, my appearance was different. When he left, I wasn't showing. When he came back, I was within weeks of having the baby. He touched my stomach, and the baby moved. He said nothing about the baby. I had nothing to say. I was ready to have the baby, and the girls were excited.

Waiting patiently, Jaiden told me he had something to give to me.

Edris

He said he had something to give me. Doesn't he realize what he has already given to me?

He gave me tears that were not out of joy; he gave me heartache, stomach pains, and loneliness. What more could he give?

I look at him, and I can't even connect with him any longer. I carry him with me always. He is my constant pain. My headache, my heartache. I thought he was my best friend. He was my second thought. My first thought was God. My first thought is GOD.

I met Jaiden in a hole in the wall. I never believed in love at first sight. I do now. I knew he was the one. The night I met him, we talked the whole night and every night afterward. I knew he would be in my life forever. Or, so I thought. I loved everything about him. I loved the way he walked. I loved the way he talked. He was articulate. I loved the fact that he was that gentle man. He opened the doors. He was amazing. He was positive.

I often studied him. On the days when he needed a true friend, I was that friend. We talked about GOD together. We cried together. We laughed together. We were together. I needed him, and I thought he needed me.

He was my second thought. My first thought was GOD. I don't know what happened. Did he wake up one day and realize I wasn't the person he gave everything to? He was my breath of fresh air.

When I looked at him, I smiled. He was my everything. I didn't care what he had to give to me. It's going to be okay. I can't cry. I am all cried out. I am numb. I am suffocating, and I am broken. I am empty. I am sad. So, what can he give? I had it all, HIM.

Dear Edris (wife),

It was almost time. We were physically apart but not mentally. I used to believe that there was nothing that would keep us apart. That's what my heart told me. I needed to be loved by somebody, not just anybody.

You might think I am saying this because I was out to sea. Sorry, you are wrong. I learned the hard way about where our marriage stands. It used to be SOLID. FIRM is an excellent way to categorize the relationship we once had. I used to think I had you in the palm of my hand. That's wrong because marriage takes two and cannot operate with only one, to be honest. I can now say I love you. I am sorry. I doubted your power. Let me explain this to you.

My love for you started like an apple seed. It grows day by day. You placed me on the ground and would water me with your love daily.

I DID NOT LOVE YOU AT FIRST. I only cared. I cared enough only to bear my apples because you showered me every day with your love. One day, you made me realize you were the person I was missing.

It was that day you did 180 degrees. You changed your attitude, clothes, and hair style. I didn't know what was happening. All I knew was that I missed the OLD YOU because there was no more water showering me with love.

As the old phrase goes, "You never know a good thing until it's gone." I learned my lesson too late. I should have borne you my shade of love from my leaves. I didn't let the apples grow bigger or redder or let the leaves grow greener.

I fell in love with you. I am in love with you. I love you more and more each day. I am sorry.

Love, Your husband

P.S. Thanks for being the woman in my life.

Edris

Thanks for being the woman in your life. I have no words for that.

I love you now. I have no words for that.

What I hear and feel is that I don't love you. I like you and care for you. I don't even have words for that.

My life has changed. No, correction: my life is changing. I prayed for you. It was supposed to be ME, YOU, and GOD.

Hearing Maxwell sing "A Woman's Work" brings me to tears.

Pray God you can cope

I stand outside this woman's work

This woman's world

Ooh, it's hard on the man

Now his part is over

Now starts the craft of the father

I know you've got a little life in you yet

I know you've got a lot of strength left

I know you've got a little life in you yet

I know you've got a lot of strength left

I should be crying, but I just can't let it show

I should be hoping, but I can't stop thinking

Of all the things I should've said

That I never said

All the things we should've done

Though we never did

All the things I should've given

But I didn't

Oh, darling, make it go

Make it go away

Give me these moments back

Give them back to me

Give me that little kiss

Give me your hand

I should be crying, but I just can't let it show

I should be hoping, but I can't stop thinking

Of all the things we should've said

That we never said

All the things we should've done

Though we never did

All the things that you needed from me

All the things that you wanted for me

All the things that I should've given

But I didn't

Oh, darling, make it go away

Just make it go away now

Songwriter: Kate Bush

Maxwell said it best. I should be crying, but I can't show. I should be hoping, but I can't stop thinking of everything we should have said that we never spoke.

I am 10 months pregnant. Any day now, I am about to have a child.

I am sure there is a lot that should have been said. Maybe, just maybe, too much was said.

I close my eyes, and I see the day he told me. I like you. **I LIKE YOU.** I will never forget how my heart stopped beating at that moment. I loved this man, and what he had for me was nothing. He had nothing for me. He was air. And he took it from me. I am suffocating.

Not happy,

Not sad;

Just empty,

Suffocating.

March 17, 1996

I spent this day in pain. We were in downtown Waikiki. We had taken the girls to walk on the beach. I was miserable and uncomfortable. I had a pair of green shorts on and my favorite K-Swiss tennis shoes. I looked ugly, and I felt ugly. I was 10 months pregnant, tired, and ready to deliver our baby.

The girls, however, were happy and excited that they were at the beach. What could be better than playing in the Pacific Ocean in Hawaii? If we were in Kansas, we would be freezing at the St. Patrick's Day Parade.

However, we were on the beach dressed in green, celebrating in our particular way. This was one of the longest days, and I wanted it to end. To the life of me, I don't remember that night. I know I was not smiling. I had nothing to smile about.

March 18, 1996

I woke up the girls around 7:30 a.m. to get ready for school. They got up and washed their faces. After they got dressed, they came downstairs for breakfast. They ate and brushed their teeth again.

I remember telling the younger one not to play in the red clay because it is the hardest to get out of clothes. She said, "Yes, ma'am," as she always does. I expect her to be covered in red clay when she comes home. From head to toe.

I walked them to the bus stop and came back home. As I walked back through the door, I felt a sharp pain down my back. I tried to act like it didn't hurt. Or at least I tried not to pay it any attention.

I recall going to the restroom; water ran down my leg. I was thinking now, maybe my water broke.

I called my closest friend, Lali, and her daughter told me she was at work. I called my girlfriend, Paula, and asked her, "How do you know you are in labor?"

To my surprise, she said, "I don't know. Lexi is adopted."

The only word I had at that moment was, "OH!" Then I softly said, "I think I am in labor. Could you please pick up the girls after school?"

After she said yes, I called Jaiden. The person who answered said he was in a meeting and asked if I could call him later. I told him, "NO! I think I am in labor and need him to come home."

He said OKAY and assured me he would be right there. I took a shower, and he was there when I got dressed. He didn't say a word. He helped me into the car and drove me to Tripler Hospital in Honolulu, HI.

The twenty-minute drive felt like an hour. I checked into the hospital. I changed my clothes, and I waited for the doctor. The doctor examined me and asked, "Have you felt any pain?"

I said, "A little."

The doctor said, "You are in labor."

I remember him telling me to walk to the third floor and back. I should be ready to have the baby then. Walking the stairs was a punishment. The more steps I took, the more pain I felt. I wanted to cry, but I kept walking, stopping, walking, and stopping. I remember Jaiden asking me if I was in pain, and I wanted to slap the hell out of him. I am sure he could read my face. He became silent.

The walk back to the room was the longest. Before I got there, I had decided not to take any meds. I didn't want the baby to have any of that.

After returning to my room, the nurse examined me and said it was time to push. Now, I wanted some meds. She said, "It is too late; the baby is here."

She said, "Lay back and push."

I pushed as hard as I could. Then, someone ordered me to try again. After that, to my surprise, the baby was here. After two pushes, I had a beautiful baby girl. I didn't want to hold her. I looked at her, and they took her away. She was 6 pounds 3.9 ounces. She was born at 6:39 p.m., and by 7:15 p.m., I was ready to eat dinner.

March 19, 1996

At midnight, I got my nerves up to see her. When I saw her, she was still covered in afterbirth, and I was upset. They immediately bathed her and placed her in my arms. I fed her a bottle, burped her, and put her back in bed. They asked me if I wanted to take her to my room. I told them, NO! They asked me if I wanted to name her. Again, I said, NO!

I wanted to rest. I heard a nurse say that they felt something was wrong. I didn't care how she felt. I tried to sleep! The nurse asked me again if something was wrong. I told her NO!

I didn't want to hold the baby. She was dirty. She asked me, "What is the baby's name?"

I told her, "Jade J White."

I had to stay an extra day for observation.

March 22, 1996

Today was the day we were finally released in beautiful Hawaii. As I looked at her, words failed me.

When I got home, I summoned my courage and called her father. At the sound of his voice, I panicked and hung up. He had no clue he had another daughter. What could I possibly say?

A week later, I tried his number again, only to find it disconnected. He had left the island without warning. Who knew when I would get another chance to reach him?

I had seen his daughter against all odds, yet we were still galaxies apart. Our future remained uncertain, but at least this journey had brought us together, even for a fleeting moment.

Dear Ryland,

I knew I would not see you today. She was born 6 pounds and 3.9 ounces today at 6:39 P.M.

Today is the beginning of life without you. She sleeps a lot right now, and she came home attached to a blanket. She drinks 4 ounces every three to four hours. She is beautiful. I'll see you in here.

I miss you, friend.

Ryland,

A week has passed since I called you. I heard your voice, and I hung up the phone. It was fear that hit me.

How do I tell you? You have a one-week-old daughter, and her name is Jade. When I see her, I see you.

I miss our talks, friend. I miss the long rides and the deep conversations.

Dear Ryland,

Jade, my six-month-old, doesn't sleep, and I'm exhausted. I wish I had someone to call to watch her so I could rest.

With two teeth, she smiles constantly, reminding me of you. Her smile is just like yours.

She's already pulling up and standing on her own. I know she'll start walking before her first birthday.

We're heading to Vegas this week. As I try to pack, she climbs into the suitcase to play.

I read to her daily, never using baby talk. I want her to learn to talk and use words early on. She recognizes her name when I say it.

She still carries her blanket and sucks a pacifier - she has to have both to be content.

September 13, 1996

Dear Ryland,

Our trip to Vegas finally happened. Jade met my mom and sister for the first time. While my sister watched her, my mom and I enjoyed a nice break at the casinos. It was great to have a little time to ourselves while the family got to know Jade.

Breaking News: Tupac just died.

In the Event Of My Demise

Dedicated to those curious

In the event of my demise

When my heart can beat no more

I hope I die for a principle

Or a belief that I had lived 4

I will die before my time

Because I feel the shadow's depth

So much I wanted to accomplish

Before I reached my Death

I have come to grips with the possibility

And wiped the last tear from my eyes

I loved all who were positive

In the event of my Demise!

Tupac Shakur

Ryland,

OMG, Ryland! The plane ride back to Hawaii was not what I wanted. I wanted her to sleep. She screamed the whole time.

We happened to be on a plane with Japanese tourists. They enjoyed her and took so many pictures of her. I am sure your baby is plastered all over Japan.

She is very independent. She knows what she wants. She loves to be outside, and we have to watch Barney when she is inside. She goes to the TV and gets the Barney tape. I have bought her every Barney tape there is.

She is seven months now, and she is actually taking steps. She calls me mommy and yells at the bottom of the steps when the girls go to bed. Of course, she has to have the binky in her mouth.

Ryland, you have no idea how I am feeling. So much has changed, and I have so much to tell you. We have a bundle of joy who rarely sleeps. You don't even know our story. I miss talking with you.

I miss you, friend. She has your smile.

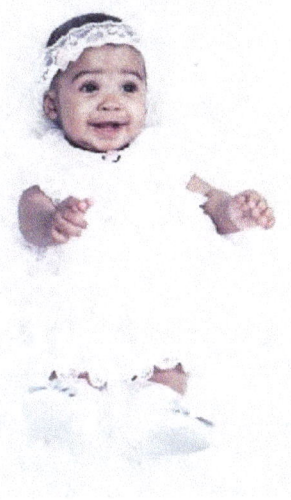

November 1996

Dear Ryland,

Guess what? She is walking now. She is eight months old, and our baby is growing up. She doesn't want to be held anymore.

I am sorry you don't know her smell, her cry. You don't know; she is part of you. She is the best of us.

She is walking now. She is saying words. She is eating table food. She only eats veggies. Her favorite foods are carrots and green beans. She is still on the bottle—my fault.

Ryland,

She is sick today, and I don't know what is happening. I can't get her to stop crying. I am holding her, and she is still crying. I am going to take her to the doctor.

Okay, she has an ear infection. She is tired from crying. Thank God she should be better in a couple of days.

Ryland, I am trying to give you pieces. I am sorry. This is life without you.

Ryland,

Jade is walking. She is eight months old, and she is cute. She is a little person taking her own steps.

Ryland,

I was sitting in the chair, watching Jade take her steps. I don't run to catch her when she falls. I let her fall on her bottom and encouraged her to get up alone. I hear him saying something about her falling.

Then the unthinkable happened. I did not see this coming. He rushed me and picked me up from the chair by my neck. I am now on my feet. I met **Terror** today. **He is bold and cold**. I am scared. I don't know what made him stop, but he did. I ran to her, and I picked her up. I wanted to cry, but I didn't. I am at a loss.

Ryland,

I am on pins and needles. I can't sleep. I am worried. I am scared. Baby girl is walking so well, but I don't want her to walk. She is just eight months old. She is still a baby. She loves Barney, the purple dinosaur. We have every VHS tape of Barney.

Ryland,

I am trying to think things out. I am wondering where you are. There is so much happening. I feel something is not right. I can't pinpoint it, though. Jade will not give up the bottle, the binky, or the blanket. I love her so much. This is life without you.

Ryland,

I just laid down from being up all night. Baby girl had just fallen asleep. Everyone is sleeping but her. I think she has her days and nights mixed up.

I was lying on the floor in front of the television. I heard footsteps coming downstairs. I rose. It was Jaiden. I asked him what he was doing. He had this look on his face that I could not place. He calmly walked over to the television and turned it off. Then he said, "DON'T WORRY ABOUT IT. DON'T WORRY ABOUT IT."

Before I could speak, he picked me up from the floor and slammed me on my back. He said, "DO I HAVE YOUR ATTENTION?"

I knew not to say a word. I kept quiet. He undressed me. Fear hit me. In my head, I thought this had to be a dream. I was scared. I quickly glanced at the baby girl's crib; she was sleeping. THANK GOD!

I didn't want him to wake her. I whimpered silently; only God heard me. I could feel the tears running down my face. How could this be? I was getting raped while my baby lay sleeping, not even five feet away.

In my mind, I said a prayer. Lord, please help me. Lord, PLEASE HELP ME!

He continued to invade my privacy. At that very moment, I died. I told him, NO! He continued to invade my privacy. He threw me around like a ragdoll. I couldn't feel my legs.

I screamed out, "Please don't do this!"

He only stopped after he climaxed. He got up. He had hit the lottery. I had lost myself. He went upstairs. I just laid there frozen until I heard the shower.

He was getting ready for work. I dressed, and I tried not to cry. I sat in the dark with tears running down my cheeks.

I heard footsteps coming down the stairs, and I immediately got sick. He walked past me, picked up his jacket, unlocked the door, and left like a typical day. I heard the car drive away. I immediately broke down and cried.

I ran to the door and chained it. I got in the shower and scrubbed my body until my skin was bleeding. I felt dirty. I felt lost. I was alone.

I dressed, approached my baby's crib, and looked at her. I remember thinking about her innocence. I picked her up, held her as close as possible, and cried. This couldn't be happening to me. This couldn't be happening to me!

WHY ME?

It was a dream, and it wasn't a dream. It was real. It happened to me.

Seasons don't change in Hawaii. In my mind, I see the change. Seasons, that is. She was born in Spring. It's December, and I don't know where you are.

Something is not right. This is life without you.

Ryland,

I have no regrets. I love this baby. She has your smile. I have you, and you don't even know it. Thank you so much. You have blessed me with much joy.

December 1996

Dear Ryland,

She is nine months old, and guess what? She woke up with chicken pox. She doesn't care, and I keep her covered with oatmeal. She has a small case. She is smiling just like you, Ryland.

She has chicken pox, and she is smiling.

Ryland,

OMG, Ryland! She STOPPED breathing today. I was watching her, and she turned blue and felt cold to the touch.

I rushed her to the hospital. They immediately took her. She screamed and yelled Mommy! Her heart is beating fast. They examined her. Finally, they let her come to me.

You won't believe it. She is now smiling. Ryland, they don't know what happened or what is wrong. They don't have any answers.

I can't sleep. I am afraid that she will stop breathing again. I lay her on my chest so she could breathe with me.

January 1997

Ryland,

I made it through the year. It was life without you. I am secretly hurting inside. I have this beautiful baby, and you don't know how beautiful she is. You don't even know she is here. I keep telling you about her smile. It matches yours.

I miss our walks, our talks. I miss my friend. Happy New Year!

February 1997

Dear Ryland,

She is eleven months old now. She is walking and saying words. She loves books. She is smart, but she still does not sleep through the night.

Next month, she will be a year old. Damn, the year went by fast. It is life without you.

Dear Ryland,

It is March 18, 1997. She is one year old. A lot has happened.

I look forward to sitting down with you and telling you what it has been like without you.

I have cried, and I have died from the inside out. Life has been challenging. I have no regrets other than life without you. WHY? You have missed her first tooth, first words, her first steps. You missed the chicken pox, the fevers, and the days she stopped breathing.

It has been life without you—365 days without you.

Her theme is Barney for her party. It is at the McDonald's in Mililani.

She knows her alphabet in Hebrew and English. Her favorite foods are what? Do you remember? Oatmeal, green beans, and carrots. Milk makes her sick. She is on the bottle but can drink from a cup.

She never cries, and she loves watching It's Bananas in Pajamas. Today, I lost her blanket at the PX. I went back and bought 5. She is still not sleeping.

Ryland,

Jade is getting sick a lot. She stopped breathing again. We rushed her to Schofield Barrack. When we got there, she was fine. Her little heart is beating fast.

I am scared, as they still don't know what is wrong.

What do I do? Who do I tell? You? Please help me.

Dear Ryland,

I try to keep my conversation with you about Jade on a positive note. So much has happened that I can't even tell you about it. I haven't reached out to you in a few months. For that, I am genuinely sorry. I have been to hell and back in the pit of the fire.

I feel like drowning and cannot get my head above the water. I often think about when you were here; we would talk, and you had a way of making things all right. I wish you were here with Jade. That's what I need.

This is life without you.

I. L. Grady

Dear Ryland,

It's a "mini you" walking behind me. I step, she steps. She smiles just like you.

I need to get off this island. I need to go home. There is no place like home. There is no place like home.

I tried to contact you. Not sure what I think you would do. This is life without you.

I got a list of Ryland A's. There are over a hundred Ryland A's, and I do not know where to begin.

Something happened. I need to go home.

Ever feel like you can't breathe?

I watch him let my baby run into the street. He didn't run after her. He didn't yell for her to stop. He just stood there.

I ran past him and grabbed her into my arms. I HAVE SOMETHING THAT MATTERS TO ME! She is my lifeline. She's my child.

I don't know what was going on in his mind when he let her run into the street. What he had done was force me into reality. She could have been hurt or maybe killed. He did not care.

I screamed at him. He looked me straight in the eye, and he was SCARED. He had this flawless record. He was a model sailor. Everyone loved him. I know no one would believe me.

In hopelessness, I went to God. I wrote a letter to a Pastor. I confessed my sins, told him, and then mailed it.

I cried. I called my mom and told her I needed to find you. I found a company that was supposed to help me find you. I got a list of 100 Ryland A's with phone numbers and addresses in the mail. I wrote an introductory letter and made plenty of phone calls.

I could not find you. I needed you to take her away with you. I needed her to be safe. I had no job and depended on someone not fond of me, and we were fighting.

JUST IN TIME. They had come with the MPs. He was removed. I felt as if GOD had answered the prayer I never prayed. The brick that was on my chest had been removed. I could breathe, at least for the moment.

I cried and told the Pastor I needed to get back home. I did not feel safe. He sat me down, and he told me what to do. He first said, "Get an order of protection," and I did.

He gave me Jaiden's Commanding Officer's home phone number. He said, "Call him every day, all day, leave messages on his phone until his messages are full."

He held my hand, and he said. "PEACE be with you."

In exactly three days, I received orders to leave. I had four tickets home. There's no place like home.

There's no place like home.

I didn't have any money. He had closed all our accounts and left me $1.37. I didn't have money to buy diapers. Crushed! I called one of my closest friends. She just sat with me and said, "We are going to have a yard sale," with the help of her twin sisters. It felt like a waiting-to-exhale moment. We sold everything but a portrait of Jesus.

Two weeks later, I was on my way home. This is life without you.

It was over, and I was relieved.

Dear Heavenly Father,

I come to you asking for forgiveness of my sins. Lord, please continue to keep me close to you. Help me on my walk, Lord. I am nothing without you. Speak to me, Lord. With all my heart, I love you. I thank you. I am nothing without you. In Jesus' name, I pray. Amen!

Ever seem like you can't breathe? Does it seem like the water is too deep? My life changed, Ryland. This is life without you.

April 1997

Ryland,

I am tired, and, of course, that little girl will not sleep. It's a nine-hour flight to Kansas, and she is not sleeping. I give up. I let her go.

She is walking up and down the aisle. Hopefully, she will give in, crawl in my arms, and sleep.

She finally does, four hours later. Now, she is sleeping pretty. She lost her binky, and I need to find it. I need that binky.

We are now in Kansas. We got off the plane in shorts and flip-flops. It's 20 degrees.

I forgot about the weather. The kids are crying that it's cold. I am laughing at them. There is only one season in Hawaii.

The girls don't remember the seasons, and Jade only knows one. Summer. Seasons change.

Dear Ryland,

I don't know where you are. It is life without you.

She is more attached to me than ever. She cries every time someone looks at her. My mother tried to pick her up, and she screamed. When I step, she steps. She is my shadow—my shadow and me.

She is getting older now. She can talk but only to me and the girls. She likes to go outside. She cried the first time she stepped on the grass.

I have put the girls in a private school. Jade and I walk to the school every day to pick them up. When Jade sees them, she runs to them with that binky in her mouth. It's nice to see her smile.

I. L. Grady

Ryland,

Today, she woke up with a temp. She just lay around all day. I gave her Tylenol. It makes her sleep. She doesn't want to eat. I try to give her fluids, and she turns her head and cries.

I took her to the doctor. She needs fluids, and she is weak. They examine her, and she has strep throat.

She had taken herself off the bottle; she didn't need it. We still have the blanket and the binky.

She feels a lot better, but she is not herself.

Ryland,

It is June. It is hot, and so is Jade. She has a fever. I gave her Tylenol.

I. L. Grady

Dear Ryland,

It has been three days, and she still has a fever. We are back to the doctor again. They can't seem to find out what is wrong.

I take her to the doctor daily, and I will keep taking her until they find out what is wrong with our baby. It's been a month now.

Ryland,

No sleep, worried, and you don't even know you have another daughter.

SCARED.

I. L. Grady

Ryland,

Today has been one of the scariest days of my life.

I rushed her to the doctor's office. She is lifeless. I am yelling at them, telling them they have to do something. They are telling me to wait.

I walk to the desk with her in my arms, and she passes out. They rush to her and grab her out of my arms. They lay her on the exam table and take her clothes off. They are yelling for ice. They are giving her a cool bath.

They have ice packs under her arms. I can't cry. I am watching what they are doing. They are trying to get her to drink. She will not drink. I tell them to give her ice. She likes ice.

Her temp is still at 104; when I brought her in, it was 101. They are telling me she is going to have to be admitted to the hospital. I asked, "When?"

They said, "Now."

Dr. Spikes says, "I have called the hospital, and they expect you to go through the ER."

She cautiously tells me she will get a spinal tap and might be unable to handle it. I let her know I am not leaving her side.

She screamed, and I didn't say a word. When they finished, I picked her up and cried until she fell asleep.

This is sleep without you.

Ryland,

It is July 4, and we are still in the hospital. Surprisingly, Jade is the only child in this hospital wing.

They are about to put an IV in her hand. They won't let me go in with her. She is screaming, "Mommy!"

I see fear in her eyes. I want to grab her out of their arms.

I follow them to the door until it closes in front of me. I sit on the floor waiting. The minutes seem like hours.

She was still crying when they put her back into my arms. She still has a temp. More lab work and X-rays tomorrow.

I. L. Grady

Dear Ryland,

It is July 5, and she is playing in a tub filled with cool water. Her temp is still high. They are giving her strong antibiotics.

I talked with the doctor. He is not telling me anything promising. I know she is about to cry again.

They have to tie her arms to her side so they can take pictures of her lungs. She has to lie still. I tell them I am going in there with her. They tell me, "No."

I tell them nicely, "I am going in there. Let's get it done."

They asked, "Where is her father?"

Tears began to fall immediately. This is life without you.

Ryland,

We have been here eight days, and she still has a temp. They tell me that a temperature means her body is fighting off something.

I need answers now. Like yesterday. She is running around like this is home. She doesn't know. It's no place like home.

I. L. Grady

Ryland,

It is day 9, and guess what? She has no temp this morning. We can go home if she can make it through Saturday night with no fever.

We spent our day walking around the hospital and reading. My mother just brought her clean blankets. I had to sneak them to be washed. I can't go without the binky and the blanket.

I am so beyond tired, Ryland.

Ryland,

Day 10. It is Sunday morning, and we have our walking papers. We are going home. My instructions are to take her temp every four hours. If her temp comes back, I must take her to the doctor.

I. L. Grady

Ryland,

It is six o'clock, and I have just taken her temp. She has a fever. We have not been away from the hospital for six hours. What am I to do? She is lifeless again. The only thing that makes her feel better is me holding her and crushed ice.

I called the hospital, and they told me to give her Tylenol and Motrin every four hours. Keep her home and take her to her doctor in the morning.

Dear Ryland,

We are the first people there. They know me by my name. They already know what is going on. The sad part about this is that Jade is used to this routine. She does not cry anymore.

The doctor examined her, and to my surprise, they had no answers. She was fine as long as she was getting meds through the IV. We can't live like this.

We can't live like this. What do I do, Ryland? This is life without you.

I am talking to you, and you can't hear me. You don't even know you have a beautiful baby girl.

Well, they have decided to put her on antibiotics therapy. Ten days. They will arrange for a nurse to come to the house. She will take her vitals and give her antibiotic shots in her thigh.

They gave her the first shot there. They numb her thigh, then give her the shot. She doesn't cry. She reached for her blanket. Every morning at 10, the nurse will come.

I. L. Grady

Ryland,

The nurse came, and she cried when she saw her. I ran and got her blanket. I sat her on my lap, and the nurse took her vitals. Then that little girl just stuck her leg out for her shot. She is getting used to it— eight more days to go.

She finished the eight days like a pro. I can go back to work now.

She is not the same baby. She has changed. She is mean. The only person she has a love for is my dad.

I tell the doctor she is not the same at her next appointment. She laughs and says that she is growing into her twos. If this is two, what will the three's be like?

Ryland,

Jade is about 18 months—time to give up the binky. I have taken it away and am about to go with the girls to St. Louis for the weekend.

I am leaving Jade with my mother and father. My father is not fond of my mother. She will eat my mother's food, but that is as far as it goes.

St. Louis was nice. We went to the zoo and some parks. We ate good food. I missed our baby.

I. L. Grady

Ryland,

When I returned from St. Louis, Jade had a brand-new binky in her mouth. I asked my mother, "Why?"

She said, "I was not going to hear her cry."

So I bought three new ones. Damn, I have to start over again.

Monday, I cut the nipple of the binky in front of her.

I told her, "Binky, all gone."

She said back to me, "Binky all gone."

I said, "Yes, binky all gone."

She cried for three days straight. By the fourth day, she had forgotten about the binky. She let the blanket go, too.

Ryland,

Jade is starting to let me go. She will not play unless I am at arm's length. She wants to play. She is battling with herself. Of course, I encourage her to play, and sometimes she does, for the most part.

I do encourage her to play with other children, but when they get close to me, she throws herself on the ground screaming. Then she gets up and tries to hit the kids.

What am I going to do with her? This is life without you.

I. L. Grady

Ryland,

It is snowing today. It is the first time she has ever seen snow. She is trying to catch the snowflakes. You should see the smile on her face.

I don't remember it ever snowing in October.

Dear Ryland,

My father is fixing Thanksgiving dinner. We have the traditional Thanksgiving dinner. I am watching what they are giving her to eat. It doesn't matter as long as it is not meat. I am almost sure they give her meat when I am not around.

She likes to watch Teletubbies on TV. In my parents' house, only Jade gets to run through the house. She runs into my father's bedroom, telling him in two words to change the TV. She says to turn it. The two words she says are to turn it. She climbs into his bed, and he moves over.

Every day, he freezes juice for her and feeds it to her. My dad expects to see Jade. Jade expects to see him also. She calls him Grand Daddy. Whenever I discipline her, he jumps in, and she runs to him. It upsets me sometimes. Those nights are the night he gets to keep her.

They get up at 5 in the morning, and she climbs into his lap. They eat and talk and laugh. I sit back and watch and smile.

This is life without you.

I. L. Grady

Ryland,

My parents haven't had a tree up since I was a child. My parents have gone out this year and bought this huge tree. When my mother puts the ornaments on the tree, Jade pulls them down and runs to the kitchen. She thinks it's a game.

My father loves this little girl. He lights up brighter than the tree. She calls him Daddy. He says, "No! Grand Daddy."

She says, " Daddy."

He says, "Grand Daddy."

Ryland,

It's her second Christmas. She has gifts up to the ceiling. She doesn't care about the gifts; she is trying to climb into my father's lap. I am trying to take her out of his lap, and she throws a fit. I leave her for some quiet time with the girls.

When I get back, she is asleep in his arms. He tells me to leave her, and she's sleeping. I tell my dad I cannot control her. She needs to spend some time with me, and I take her while she is asleep. At night, she cries for my dad. She gets up at 5 a.m. expecting to see him. I make it a point for her to see him before I go to work.

This is life without you.

I. L. Grady

Ryland,

    She is about to be in her terrible two-stage. Actually, she is already. They say kids bite because they can't express their thoughts. She can talk. Why is she naughty?

Ryland,

Forgive me. I haven't reached out to you. It's hard. I can't touch you. I can't see you.

I. L. Grady

Ryland,

Guess what? She is two today. I bought her another Barney cake. Yes, she still loves Barney. I didn't get her anything for her birthday. We took pictures and blew out the candles on the cake.

My father took her to Kid Quest to play. He stayed all day just watching her play. She is Grand Daddy's little girl.

Ryland,

If I had to tell you what is on my mind, it would be that she has been sick on and off. What warms my heart is that she smiles through her pain. If I didn't know our child, you would never know she is sick.

She smiles in her sleep. How beautiful is that? When she cries, she cries.

I still do not let her sleep by herself. Her breathing still scares me. I need her close to me. There is nothing more frightening than seeing your baby stop breathing. She has; she did. It scared me.

I. L. Grady

Ryland,

This is life without you.

I don't know where you are. It's been three years since I last saw you. Nothing has changed. I am still your friend.

Nothing has changed. I still think of you daily, and our joy is growing. She is a tiny daredevil.

She looks just like you. I look at her, and I see that smile of yours.

Ryland,

I have the opportunity to take her to work with me. It helps in two ways. Daycare, and I get to have her close to me.

We get up every morning and fight to eat, put our clothes on, and brush our teeth. After I put her jacket on, it is a go. She runs, grabs her backpack, and jumps in the car seat. As I fasten her in, I wonder if the little girl will ever go out of it. She is three, and she still wears 18 months' clothes. I take her to the doctor, and they smile and say, "Look at the mama."

That brings me some comfort, but my nickname growing up was Midget. She is my little helper.

I work for Hallmark Cards. I have the Midwest Regional stores, so we pack our overnight bags every other week and leave for Texas, Wichita, Kansas, or Missouri. The ride is always lovely because she sleeps.

I. L. Grady

Ryland,

She has a full mouth of teeth. Her smile still amazes me. She is quiet but not shy. She still does not allow people in her space.

Guess what? She still takes a nap. I can lay her down after lunch, about 1 o'clock, and she will sleep for at least two hours. That is my "me time." I can get my paperwork done.

I find myself staring at her. I just say, "He misses her and doesn't even know it. Our baby."

Ryland,

I read to her every night. She goes to the bookshelf and gets a book. Green eggs and Ham. Every night, we read Green Eggs and Ham.

I. L. Grady

Ryland,

Since she is having oral surgery this coming Tuesday to fix issues with her teeth, you would be here if you knew about it. Her mouth is always wet. The dentist tells me she needs to get some of those teeth out.

She is laughing and smiling. She doesn't even know she is about to be taken out of my arms.

They come to get her in a red wagon. They seem to think she is going to follow them. No! Not this baby. They walk towards her, and she runs in the opposite direction. She is reaching for me, and they are pulling her away. I kiss her on her forehead.

Ryland,

I waited three long hours. When she finally woke up, she reached for me. I climb into bed with her until it is time to go. They wheeled us out, personally put her in the car seat, and gave her a blanket. She grabs it and lays her head on it. She sleeps on the ride home. I thank Tee for being there with me.

This life without you.

I. L. Grady

Ryland,

It is time for her to start school. Preschool. I have been blessed with having her with me. I want to do something different—a new job offer. I want to go back to school. I am worried. I have never been without her.

Mr. Ryland,

I got the job. I am in school. The hard part is putting her in school. I found two schools. Denaro and Lindsay. I chose Lindsay.

I took her to see her school. She hides behind me. She will not look at the principal. I can hardly ask questions. The principal says she is spoiled. In my mind, I say, well, yeah. Out of my mouth, I tell her I am all she knows.

She must have read something on my face. She immediately stood up and assured me it was going to be okay. She will be okay. She will be okay. That should be music to my ears, but my mind told me something different.

I. L. Grady

Ryland,

I have to start this job. She's still not in school. I have paid for her tuition, and she has not stepped foot in the school. I have to take her.

Ryland,

It's my first day at work and Jade's first day of school. She has a navy blue skirt and a white shirt—black shoes with white socks. I have not ordered her uniform yet. As we walked, she held my hand tight. I can see the fear in her eyes.

I walk her to her room and sit with her, trying to encourage her to play so I can make my grand exit. It doesn't work, but I have to go.

Her teacher is Ms. Slaughter. She takes her from me, and she screams and cries. My heart is broken. As I am walking out, I dare not look back. I feel her crying. I am crying, too. I leave the building, sit in my car, and tears begin to fall.

This life without you.

I. L. Grady

Ryland,

    It has been three months since Jade started school. She cries all day. It doesn't matter what time of day; I call to check on her, and she is crying. They tell me she is okay. It just breaks my heart to see her so unhappy.

Ryland,

Guess what? I dropped Jade off today, and she said, "Bye, Mommy."

She didn't cry. She just said, "Bye, Mommy."

She walked away with Imani as if she had done this every day. I can't believe this. She said, "Bye, Mommy."

It took her three months to get to where she is today. She is smiling, and so am I. I am smiling at her.

I. L. Grady

Ryland,

She is her usual self. I picked her up, and the teachers told me she was intelligent and outgoing.

I pick her up in my arms even though she can walk. I even carried her to the car. In my head, I am saying, *"Whom are they talking about? That*'s not my child."

They haven't seen her true colors. I know my child.

Ryland,

It is December, and I wonder how my friend is. Jade is four years old and mean. I wonder where this little girl comes from.

She is beautiful, and she has your smile.

Daddy Ryland,

The real Jade has just stood up. I received a call around 9:00. I just dropped her off at 7:30 this morning, and everything was fine.

A teacher called me and told me my four-year-old was suspended from school. At first, this did not register with me. She is four. How does a four-year-old get put out of school? I said, "Okay."

I am listening to what happened. As I hear, I say this story must be made up. Jade asked to do devotions. The teacher told her no and told her to sit down. Jade told her no. Jade said, "Alicia always does the devotion."

Then, she told the teacher that Alicia was not God's only child. This upsets the teacher, and she grabs Jade's arm and drags her out of class. Jade then tells her to call the police or call her momma.

She calls me, and I ask, "Who does devotion every day?"

She tells me, Alicia. I told her I would call her back. I called her back and was told that Jade could stay in the office for the rest of the day. I replied and said, "You all are out of your mind. I am coming to get her."

I asked Tee to pick her up. When the office manager came in, she asked, "Is Jade sick?"

Terry said he was asked to pick up Jade because she was suspended. She had no idea what had happened. She did not know why she was suspended from school.

Tee reached for Jade, and he saw handprints on her arm. Now he is mad. Jade is suspended, but she has a handprint on her arm.

Tee calls me, and when I answer the phone, Jade is in the background saying, "Call the police, call the police!"

Tee takes her home, and I get a call from the school when I arrive. "Edris, please come to school in the morning and bring Jade."

I asked her, "Why does my child have a handprint on her arm?"

She said nothing. She apologized and said we would talk in the morning.

I didn't say anything to Jade about what happened. Mommy's got this one. The little girl is strong-minded. When she talks, you wonder if she is four. If you only knew. You have a treasure.

Ryland,

The next morning, Jade and I went to the school. She was her usual self, hanging onto me. Mind you, she is more than likely forgotten about yesterday.

When we walked in, all the teachers were in the office. They were having the morning meeting, which they have every morning before commencing their class. The teacher who grabbed her arm came rushing out of the office.

She didn't say anything to me. She went straight to Jade. She got on her knees and said. "Please, forgive me! Please forgive me. I am sorry."

Why would a teacher get on her knees and beg a four-year-old? I pulled Jade away from her. I told her, "Don't you ever call me again unless she is not well. You don't give a four-year-old power over you. Jade runs that class, not you, and I wish you well. Then I left.

Ryland,

It's the end of the school year, and they did not call me for ANYTHING! I was serious, and they knew it. I still laugh, "Call the police." That little girl!

I. L. Grady

Ryland,

It has been a long time since we touched base. School is over, and I need a place for Jade to go. I have to travel with this job. I have decided to send her to my sister.

They go every summer to help my sisters with the twins. My mother and I drove the girls to Denver, CO. I brought the food they liked and left them money to help my sister.

Ryland,

Jade had been gone a week, and I was surprised when I called; she did not cry. My sister informed me she has Jade on a schedule. She wakes her up in the morning. She does not get to sleep in. She eats breakfast. She plays, and after lunch, she takes a nap.

Fine with me. Whatever works.

I. L. Grady

Ryland,

I wonder what you are doing? I am trying to stay positive and strong. This thought process is draining. I miss our talks. I miss our walks. I miss seeing that smile on your face that makes my day.

Today, I am on my way to get our daughter. I didn't call my sister. I just got in the car and drove eight hours straight.

The girls called me and told me my sister had her sit at the table all day because she would not eat Malt-O-Meal. Jade just stayed there. She didn't cry, but she would not eat. She was forced to stay at the table the whole day and half the night without food. I was furious. I brought her food to eat.

When I got there, she ran to me. She had your smile, which made me smile. I kissed her. My sister told me how Jade would not follow directions. I heard her, but I wasn't listening.

The following day, we left, and in my heart, I knew she would never return.

Ryland,

I am taking Jade to work with me. She will be in Kindergarten when school starts. I work at Research Medical Center as a regional manager for Laurie Gifts. My job is to set up the shop and install the computers. I hire and train the managers and help them with the grand opening.

You should see Jade. It is incredible how smart she is. She knows how to run the computer. She has watched me do this repeatedly, and she knows it by heart. She is my joy. I watch her tell my crew how to do their job. She is a breath of fresh air. The customers love her.

I. L. Grady

Ryland,

It's time for her to go to school. The girls are back from my sisters. I wonder what kind of year we are going to have. They say that she is ready for 1st grade. I decline. I have decided to let her enjoy being a kid. She has the same teacher. I wonder what this year is going to be like. There is always a story to be told.

Ryland, please forgive me. I have not told you earlier what has been going on. I am working. Jade is being a kid, and I miss my friend. The school has started, and to my surprise, I am not having any problems so far. Please cross your fingers, as I have crossed mine. She is reading, writing, and doing math. She is becoming a big girl.

I get many notes that I do not take to heart. It seems as if she wants to teach the class. I can't help her. She was the one who got on her knees. I do tell Jade the importance of school.

Ryland,

I have been in a meeting all day, and that little girl is in an uproar. I taught her my work number. What did I do that for? She has called me at least four times. I told her not to call me again today. I told each one of them to work it out. I hung up the phone.

My meetings are over, and to my surprise, I didn't get another call. I left work, glad to be on my way home. I made a left on my street, and my heart stopped. I saw two police cars at my house. I jumped out of the car and ran to my house without closing the door. There were two police officers on the porch. They told me to calm down; everything was okay.

I had to brace myself for what I was about to walk into. Walking in, I saw my nieces sitting on the couch with their heads down. Jade is on the phone talking to 911. Jade roared loudly, "It was an emergency. The Bible says to obey your mother and father. It doesn't say to obey your sisters."

My mother told me to handle it. Jade said, "They were trying to whoop me. It was an emergency".

The police were laughing, but I wasn't. After all the laughter, they asked Jade not to call the police on her sisters. Officer Paul gave her his cell number and told her to use it. She said, "Thank you."

After they left, I sat on the couch and looked at my little family. That was the last time Jade stayed home with them. I knew she would call the police on them.

I. L. Grady

Ryland,

She is in a play, and she knows all of her lines. She will be performing in front of at least 200 people. She is an angel—one of six.

You should have seen her and the angels. They are battling over the microphone. Guess who won? Yes, Jade. You should see her facial expression. It's to die for. Smiling. She has character.

This is life without you.

Ryland,

Thank you so much for her. You don't even know you have her. She would be the apple of your eye. She would make you smile as she does me.

I look at her while she sleeps; she brings me so much PEACE. Thank you again.

I. L. Grady

Ryland,

What do I say? She made it through another year. She is dressed in her cap and gown. She knows her line. She is the MC. She has grown at least four inches.

I didn't think she would ever get out of the car seat. Now, she is in a booster seat. She looks like you more and more. What do I do?

We had a delightful summer. We traveled and just hung out. She has given up the dresses. She is a tomboy.

She is learning to ride a bike without training wheels. She falls, and she falls, and she falls. Her arms are bruised, and her legs are all scratched up. She gets back on that bike, and she does it again. She still smiles when she is not feeling well. You would never know she's sick.

I love this little girl. She is my joy. I love this little girl. I love her so much.

This is life without you.

Ryland,

I haven't reached out to you in a while. Not because I don't want to. I want you to know that.

She has excellent conversations. Her imagination is fantastic. When I go up to the school, she is always with somebody. They love this little girl. She is spoiled, I would say.

They constantly get on her about keeping her shoes on. I tell them we don't wear shoes in our house; we take them off at the door.

She knows her Bible well. She learns her verse. I wish I could get her to sit up straight. She constantly lies on her desk. She dislikes her uniform, which I love. I don't pay her any attention. When we get home, it is the first thing she pulls off after the shoes.

She is riding a bike now with no training wheels. She doesn't realize that the training wheels are still on but not touching the ground. She has been riding without wheels for weeks. Guess who put the first dent in my car? She could not stop the bike. She fell, I ran to her, and I picked her up off the ground. You guessed it; she was smiling—that girl of ours.

She is strong, and you can see her muscles in her arms. Her grades are excellent. She is way above grade level. She likes books, and every month, she spends whatever she wants on books. It's my treat to her. I remember his favorite book. Green Eggs and Ham.

I. L. Grady

Ryland,

This year she had a lovely party. We put on her cake, PUSH, Praying Until Something Happens. I had her give gifts instead of receiving them. She is a blessed child.

This is life without you.

She is small but getting taller. I look at her while she sleeps, and she smiles. I wonder if the angels are watching over her.

Of course, they are.

Dearest Ryland,

Tonight, I thought about you, and in my mind, I wondered if you were okay. I think about whether you are married and happy. I pray every night that you are out of harm's way.

You have a beautiful daughter. She looks like you so much. She has your smile. If you knew what I knew, you would be so proud. You would love her as I do. She would make you smile.

I. L. Grady

Good morning,

If there is one thing I could tell you about Jade, it would be her drive to win. She wants to do her best and always be her best. Every night, I ask her who the most crucial person in the world is. I tell her to say I am. She says, "God."

I ask her who is going to make the difference. She says, "God."

I say, "I am!"

She says, "God."

She knows who is in charge. Yep! It is GOD.

Ryland,

Today, I scolded her about Bobby. She cried and got mad. I didn't scold her because she was defending herself. I was on her because she really wanted to hurt him. She jumped on this boy, and she would not stop hitting him. I am not in the mood to fight Bobby's mom. I think Bobby has a big headache.

I got a call about Bobby and listened to what they said. They never mentioned he was pulling her hair or calling her names. I let them talk. Then, I asked them if they were done. "Yes, we are done."

I said, "Okay, I have to get back to work."

Then, I hung up the phone.

This is my life without you.

I. L. Grady

Hey you,

I wish I knew where you were. I travel a lot now and have to leave her quite often. She cries a lot. I know she is missing me because I miss her.

My mother does not have kids, so I have to depend on others for her care. It is not music to my ears when I call her and hear her call someone else mom. At times, she does not want to go home. I cry.

This is life without you.

You should see her now. She has beautiful brown eyes to go with that smile. Her complexion is perfect. She is actually shy. She doesn't talk much. If you ask her a question, she will answer it. She doesn't have a circle of friends. She loves to go to church.

Ryland,

I have to say your name. It gives me great comfort. It is my way of reaching out to you. I am calling you, and I know you are not there. I have a lot to tell you, Ryland.

She sings in the choir and volunteers for anything open. The way she dresses has changed. I am smiling because she is so not like me. She is all you.

She is into lip gloss now. She is growing up. She is combing her naturally curly hair. I lay my head on her lap, and she brushes my hair, eyes, and forehead. She tells me in her cutesy voice, "Mommy, you so pretty."

It makes me smile that she takes the time to look at me.

I. L. Grady

Ryland,

I have had the pleasure of raising your child. She is fantastic. She works hard for the things she wants.

It is funny how life changes things. I never wanted a child. I was happy with taking care of other people's kids. Never in my wildest dreams did I think I would have a child. I have you to thank, regardless of the outcome. It happened, and I have no regrets.

This is life with you.

Ryland,

I get more calls from her school now. It's that book, the student conduct book. She knows that book from front to back. She is swift to tell you when something is not done correctly.

She has Mrs. Perry as her teacher. I am not happy with this teacher. Can she teach? We all can teach, right? I would not say I like the way she talks to the children. I made it a point to tell Jade to call me anytime. Honestly, I show up without informing them. I am often asked if something is wrong. I tell them nothing to fear if they are doing things right.

I. L. Grady

Ryland,

She writes me notes every day. Most of the time, it is just about what happened that day or a silly joke. She has no idea she is doing so many things in one. This helps her; it is her power, and she doesn't even know it yet.

To my Lord. I am nothing without you. I thank you for my many blessings. You walked with me when I knew I was alone. I am nothing without you. Speak to me, Lord. Speak to me, Lord. I need you. In Jesus' name, I pray.

Ryland,

It's been a long time since I have written to you. Jade has transformed into a lovely girl. She loves clothes. It's probably my fault. I require her to be her best. Look her best at all times. I am proud of her.

She has a journal of her teachers. She got mad one day, and she told them. They called me, and I told them you don't have to worry about it if you are not doing anything wrong. I read the journal only when she has a bad day. Believe me, she is very detailed. She leaves nothing out.

I. L. Grady

Ryland,

She had another bad day at school. I usually let her try to work it out, but today, I have to take a trip to the school.

Ms Palls, in a kids' world, would be called a bully. She has a problem with my child, and it is getting old. So, I guess today we are going to have some grown-up conversations. Right is right, no matter how you twist it—no playing small.

Today, I am fed up. I tried hard not to give her a piece of my mind. Leave my child alone.

Guess what happened? I got pulled into the principal's office. The principal asked me to talk with her, and I did. Ms Palls is in the office as well. Ms Palls vaguely expressed herself, and I did as well. She says what is on her mind. I stood up, looked her in the eyes, and said, "Look, I don't play with kids, and I am not playing with you."

The principal stands up between us and says, "Okay, okay, let's pray."

We prayed, and when we were done, I told her, if you touch my child or talk to my child crazy again, you will have to deal with me.

This is life without you.

Ryland,

I feel lost today. I am sad, and I want to cry. This is becoming unbelievable. For years, it has been my child, my child. She has a father who has no idea. She is carrying his smile. She looks like him. She smiles like him, and he doesn't know she is here. I am sad.

This is life without you.

This year has been so much rewarding. She started competing in many things. She is out to win everything. She wants first place, and you know, I believe her. She is going to win.

She loves school. She doesn't want to miss school even when she is sick.

You go, girl! Go, get it.

I. L. Grady

Ryland,

Jade's best friend is Drea. They have been best friends since they were four years old. Both of them started school on the same day. Both of them were crying.

Jade never ran out of school. Drea did. She would run out of the building crying to her grandmother, "Let's pray! Let's pray!" and she would. Today, both of them want to go skating.

Now, they want to go to the movies. This will be the first time she has ever gone anywhere without me. Let's see if I can make it through the day.

Mr. Ryland,

Guess what? I made it. I made it through the day without my baby girl. What was so sweet was that she ran to me and thanked me for letting her go. She was happy and smiling. I love that little girl.

Her birthday is in a few weeks. She wants skates. I am sure she will get them. She is growing up before my eyes.

I hate that I miss you, and I can do nothing about it, Ryland. You know that some bonds last forever; they cannot be broken. Friend, I have that with you.

March 18th is her birthday. She was born at 6:30 PM and weighed 6 pounds 3.9 ounces. I think I will play those numbers.

I bought her a pair of black skates. She is a big girl now. Every Saturday, she goes skating from 7 to 11. I sometimes wait outside in my car for her to come out. I must admit that I am often nervous. My little girl is growing up, and it is scary.

I forgot to tell you. She won 1st place in the Science contest.

I have never given her a birthday party. She can't miss something she never had. I keep telling myself that.

I tell her she is so blessed, so we give her gifts to a child in need instead of receiving them. She doesn't seem to mind. I promise you she never goes without anything. She is very blessed, and she knows it.

Around this time every year, I think of you quite often. It's her birthday, and I hope it will be as special to you as it is to me. She is growing taller, and she is beautiful. I am not saying that because she is my baby girl. She is actually beautiful.

I. L. Grady

She is beautiful.

Ryland,

The school will be out in a couple of months. I am enrolling Jade in summer school. I put her in school all year round. So far, it doesn't bother her.

My grandmother died today. Jade never got to meet her. I am leaving in a couple of days to go to Mississippi. I decided not to take her.

I showed pictures of Jade. I am not surprised that they asked about you. Is her father Hawaiian? No, her father is black. The questions are beginning to get on my nerves.

We have a beautiful baby girl. She has a unique look. Beautiful. She walks tall. When I look at her, I see you. She is a little mean and a little sweet. She is ours, and you don't even know.

This is life without you.

She wears the perfect makeup—a smile.

Ryland,

Guess what? I am about to take my first trip out of the country. Mexico.

I am excited, but my baby will be left in Kansas. She doesn't even care that I am leaving. I will be gone for nine days.

It would be so nice if I knew where you were. I could drop her off and then pick her back up. Knowing that she would be safe in her father's arms would be settling.

Do I have to repeat it? It's life without you.

Mexico

I love it here in Mexico. I am getting a lot of sunshine and have met many people from diverse backgrounds. I shopped, and I tried my best not to call her.

Sorry that I couldn't resist and I called her. My baby girl had a good time without me. I bought her T-shirts, purses, and bracelets— and brought her me. She was happy to see me. I missed her dearly.

Disney World

I promised her a trip to Disney World. I saved for two years for this trip. It was her week, and we did everything she wanted to do. I took pictures, and she was so pretty with her curly hair and braces.

Ritzy saw me looking at her pictures. I told her she was my lifeline.

I. L. Grady

Ryland,

Every year, I look for you. This year, I pointed my browser to www.peoplefinders.com and think I have found you. I put in your name, and I knew I had found you.

Ryland A. It was the A that stood out—Ryland from Virginia. I remembered your unique middle name. I remembered you were from Virginia. It was you. I knew it in my heart. It was you. I felt sick to my stomach, and I couldn't breathe, but I was breathing. I found my friend. I found the person who told me I was loved and believed him.

Jade saw your name on a piece of paper on the table. Mommy, who is Ryland? He is a family member. Mommy, how is he a family member? Jade, he is just a family member.

Ryland A.,

I went to the drugstore and got you a card saying, "It's a girl." I held onto it. Then I put it away. It did not feel right.

The card didn't feel right. So I wrote you a letter instead. As I wrote the letter, I cried. I knew I had found you. I didn't know if you were married. I didn't know if you had kids.

I couldn't send the card. What if your wife got your mail? How would she react? How would she feel? It seemed like a lifetime. But I had found you. I had found the person who gave me life. I knew where you were.

Then fear hit me.

This is my life without you!

"Our deepest fear is not that we are inadequate. Our deepest fear is that we are powerful beyond measure. It is our light, not our darkness that frightens us."

–Nelson Mandela.

I. L. Grady

Hello, Mr. Ryland A.,

It has been a long time since we have touched base. I am sure you never thought you would hear from me.

How are you doing?

I have gone through this very moment in my head many times. I have tried on several occasions to locate you.

Do you remember the last meeting we had? You left a note on my car. You said in a two-page letter that you were afraid, in so many words, about me being pregnant. You were about to retire and could get into trouble if they found out you were with an enlisted man's wife.

I understood everything you were feeling. We got caught up in the moment. You were going through things with Vitisha. You all had broken up. At that time of your life, you were a hot mess.

We were friends. We would talk for hours, mainly about Vitisha and being away from home. No one believed we were just friends.

Well, for that reason, I am writing to you.

We have a 13-year-old daughter. I bet you're wondering why I am telling you now.

1. Thirteen years ago, you couldn't handle it;

2. I didn't want you to lose your retirement, and

3. You have the right to know your daughter.

   She looks just like you.

   I am not looking for anything. I am doing the right thing, and I am okay with that. I would like you to call me so we can talk about it.

You can always contact me at (555) 272-5963 or leave me a message by contacting my mother at (555) 206-6959.

Please, contact me!

Sincerely,

Edris L.

PS: I mailed this letter on Monday, and by Wednesday, the phone rang. It was you. It was no longer life without you. I said, "Hello."

You said, "Hello, Edris."

You asked, "What is our daughter's name?"

"Jade," I said as tears rolled down my cheeks.

This was life with you.

Jade

She was born at Tripler Hospital in Honolulu, Hawaii. She was six pounds and 3.9 ounces. I had no idea how to tell her about the man who gave her life. She does not know him. He means nothing to her; she is a mirror image of him.

It was life without him, and it was life without her.

Ryland and I talked every day. We decided that it was time to tell her who Ryland was. I asked her to sit with me so we could talk. Then, I asked her if she remembered when she asked me about a man named Ryland. She said, "Yes."

I said to her, "Ryland is your father."

She cried. I just looked at her, not knowing what to do. She raised her head and said, "Do I have to go to school tomorrow?"

I told her, "No."

That was it. The hardest thing in my life turned out to be the easiest thing.

LIFE WITH HIM

I dreamed of this day. I hoped for this day when our life would be LIFE with you. I dreamed of how she would meet you. What would you say? What would she say? What would I say?

On April 24th, we got on a plane for Washington, D.C., and the whole journey, I prepared my mind to meet you face to face.

Once the plane landed, tears began to fall. I was crying. They were tears of joy. I no longer question everything I did in life since before March 18, 1996.

I thought you would be the Ryland of fourteen years ago. You weren't. You had changed. It is funny how things change, how people change. Indeed, things don't stay the same.

You were no longer the slim Ryland I remembered. You were fit and muscular. You greeted me with a hug and then hugged her. Jade just hid behind me, and she did not say a word. You asked her about God, and she replied with:

"Honor thy father and mother as the Lord God commanded thee that it be well with thee and that thou mayest live long." (Exodus 20:12).

She amazes me. I did not expect that. I love her so much. God is good.

The whole week, we took time to learn about each other. We talked and took long walks together. It was 13 years we had to catch up on.

One night before bed, you asked Jade, "Who am I?"

She replied, "My Dad."

"Call me that then," you said.

At that point, it was the beginning of life with you.

135

LIFE WITH YOU

You have been understanding. I often look back on the person I was years ago. I ask myself what I would do differently. My answer to you is NOTHING. In my heart, I knew from the day I found out I was pregnant that I loved my child. What I didn't realize was your heart.

This situation in life wasn't fair, and it sometimes hurt. I recall how easy it was for me to tell you. I had no worries, and I don't know why. I am worried about you … and your well-being.

I understood the letter that you wrote me. What captured my thoughts was your distress. I read your letter with the understanding that this was a life-changing situation. I am about to bring a child into this world, and this will be life without you.

I called my friend (YOU) and left a message on your phone telling you not to worry. I walked out of your life as quickly as I walked in. I entombed our every thought, talk, and walk. It was over, and my life was about to take the beat of a different drum.

LIFE WITH YOU

That's what it has not been: life with you. It was life without you.

I am unsure how long I would travel down that road. I was driving. I didn't have any stops or forks on the road. I was driving. I believed that I could do this by myself. I thought I had no choice. It wasn't easy, and I don't know if I had something to prove. I know I wasn't trying to show you that I didn't need you because I did.

I needed you every breath she didn't take. It was fear that hit me. FEAR!

I carried fear throughout my life, fearing what you might feel or think. I have your life, your daughter, in my hands.

JD talked with me and put my mind at ease. He said, "If I were him, I would want to know I have a daughter."

He gave me peace of mind by thinking maybe you want to know. It was at that point that I knew that it was okay. I step out on faith. Fear no longer had me. I needed it to be all right. It has been life without you. I didn't plan on bringing a child into this world as I have. She is all I have, and she is my AIR. She is part of you. This is no longer life without you.

THIS IS LIFE WITH YOU!

Dear Ryland,

First of all, I would like to say I love you. Please don't take this the wrong way. I love you because you are the father of my child. I feel it will be our love and respect that will keep our child-centered. Unlike other relationships, we have something special because we were not a couple. We were friends who got caught up in a moment.

Now, we have Jade. I didn't plan on bringing a child into this world, but it happened. Your reaction didn't ever anger me. I understood. You had something to lose, Ryland.

I want you to understand my actions as far as our daughter. I decided to have her because she was a life created, and we had no right to take her life based on fear. You have to understand that you were my valued friend, and I realize now that you didn't know how I felt for you. If you knew, you would have known; I would have never brought harm to you. You didn't want the baby, and I didn't want you to feel betrayed, so I did what I felt was right.

I had nothing to gain then or now. The difference now is that I am older. I have tried to find you on several occasions. Many times, it was fear that kept me from going on with the process. My heart was so in tune with what you might think that I forgot about our baby.

Don't get me wrong. I gave Jade the best I could give her. I taught her to hold her head high and never let anyone take her joy. She did nothing wrong. She didn't ask to be born and has every right to know who she is. Her father, Ryland, had every right to know the life that he had created.

I never forgot about you. Look at her. How could I? On her 13th birthday, I found your address. I first bought you a card that said, "It's a girl." Then, I wrote you a letter that would change the rest of my life. Monday, I dropped it in the mailbox and walked away. Wednesday, I received a call from you, and we are here.

I don't want anything from you other than a father's love for his child. Our daughter needs her father. I like your input and advice. I don't want to parent alone anymore. I need you.

I hope you realize I am not trying to reap any benefits. I have the most valuable gift, our daughter. This happened for a reason, and I am grateful for the time and effort. I am excited about Jade's future and who she will become.

Thank you for everything,

Edris

Imagine This

When I started this, it was not a writing venture. It was my most intimate thought to a well-deserving friend. It was at a point in my life when everything made no sense. It was the beginning of my life.

There is no greater love than the love of two, meaning parents working on all cylinders. You have two loving parents who both adore their daughter.

Every day should be good for you, no matter how upset you become. Remember, time will not wait until your madness goes away, then start again when you are calm. Every minute you are mad and upset about anything, life will pass you by. The rat race of life goes on with or without you, so decide every day whether you are a rat or a fat cat on the sidelines ... you have choices! Select them carefully and with a positive outcome.

I. L. Grady

"I had lost my words

I had lost my action

I had lost my presence

I had lost my feelings

I had lost my hope

I had lost everything in search of you

But I haven't found anything, and

even I had lost myself completely."

Unknown author

Thank you

Michelle and Lexi for quietly helping me with my adventure

www.ingramcontent.com/pod-product-compliance
Lightning Source LLC
Chambersburg PA
CBHW071154120626
46546CB00006B/2268